MW00957776
This book
belongs to:

Christmas
BRAIN TEASERS
Activity Book for Kids
Stocking Stuffers for Kids

Published by Thomas P. P.

ISBN: ________________

Printed in the USA

MAZE #1

MAZE #2

MAZE #3

MAZE #4

MAZE #5

MAZE #6

MAZE #7

MAZE #8

MAZE #9

MAZE #10

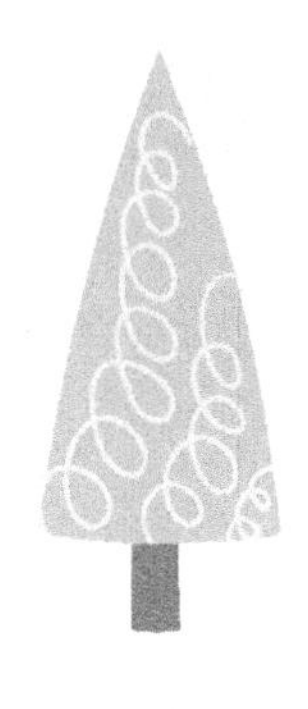

MAZE #11

MAZE #12

MAZE #13

MAZE #14

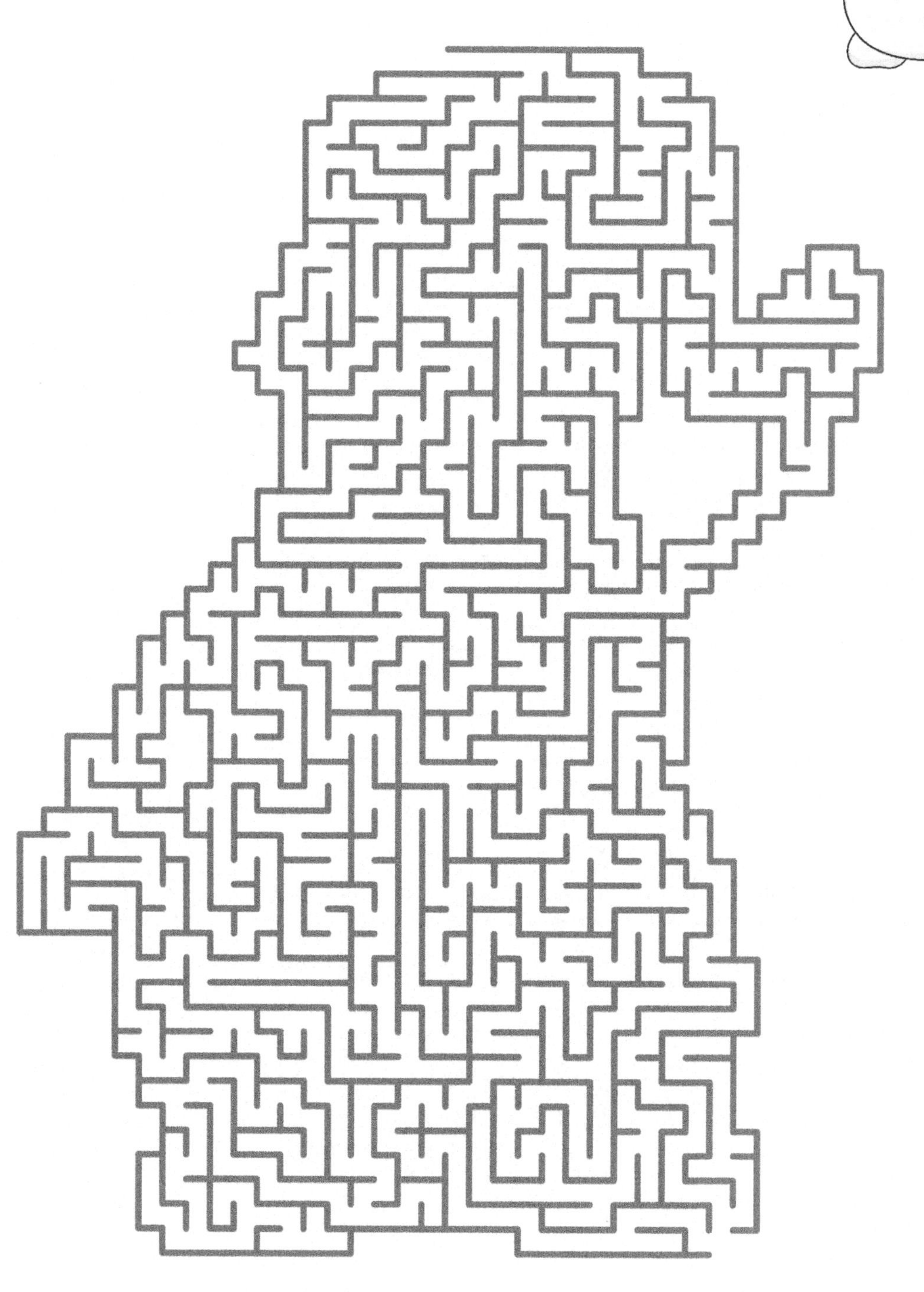

MAZE #15

MAZE #16

MAZE #17

MAZE #18

MAZE #19

MAZE #20

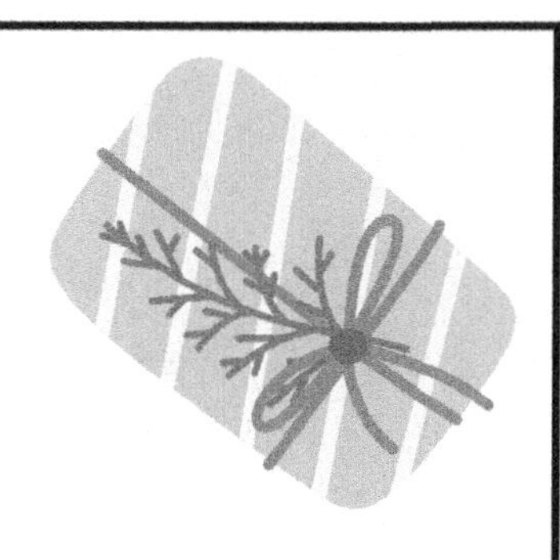

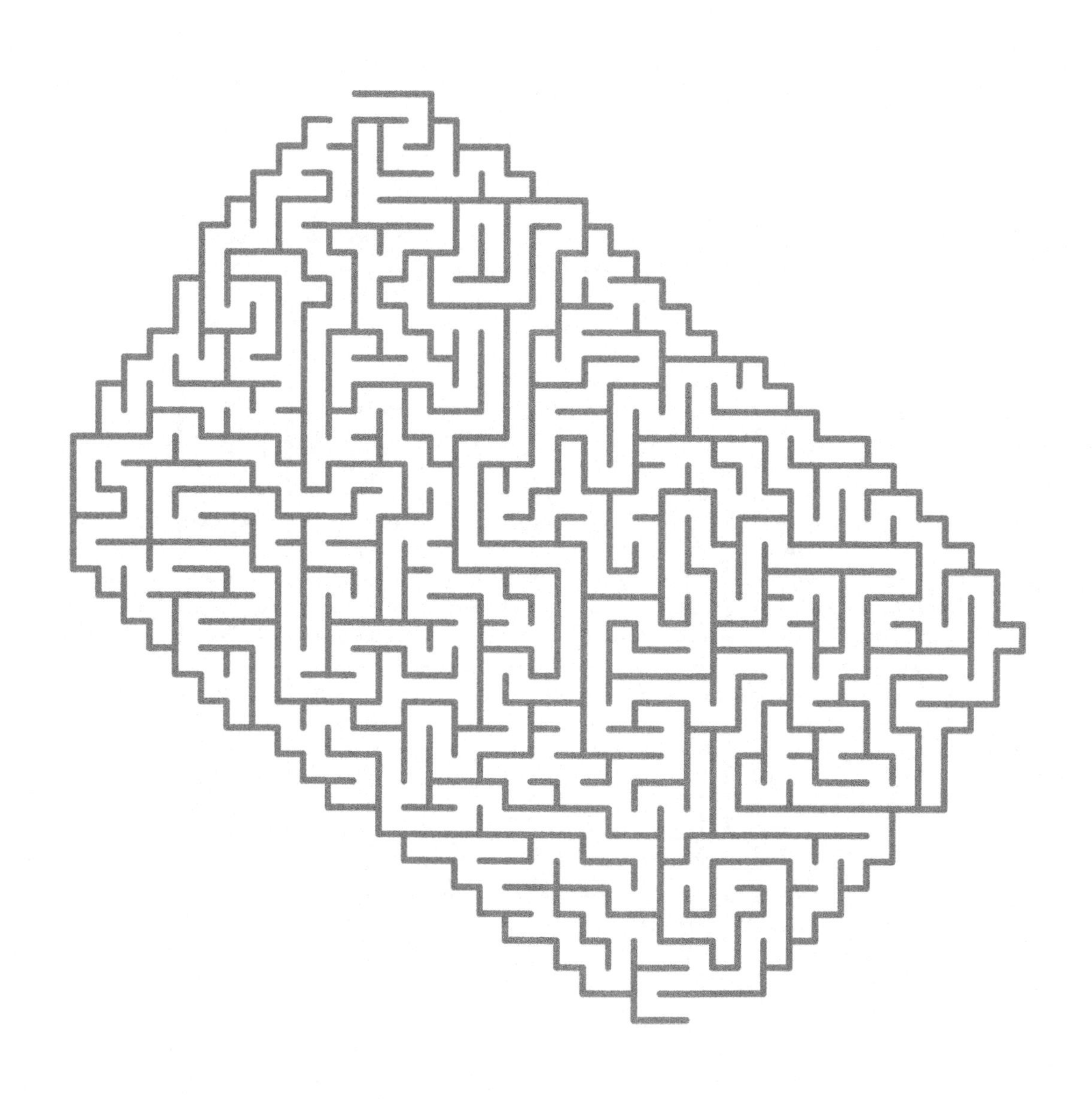

MAZE #21

MAZE #22

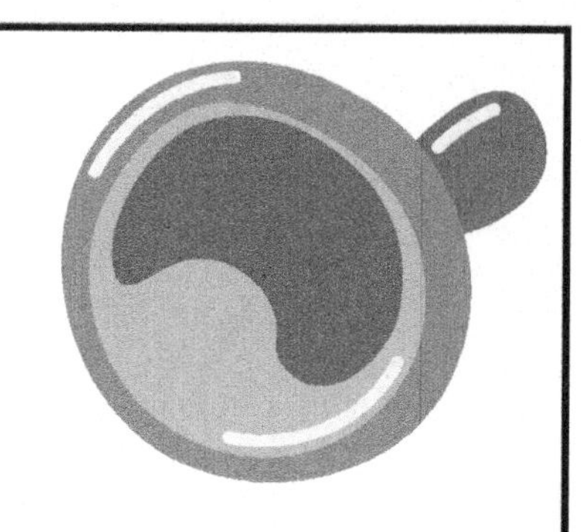

MAZE #23

MAZE #24

MAZE #25

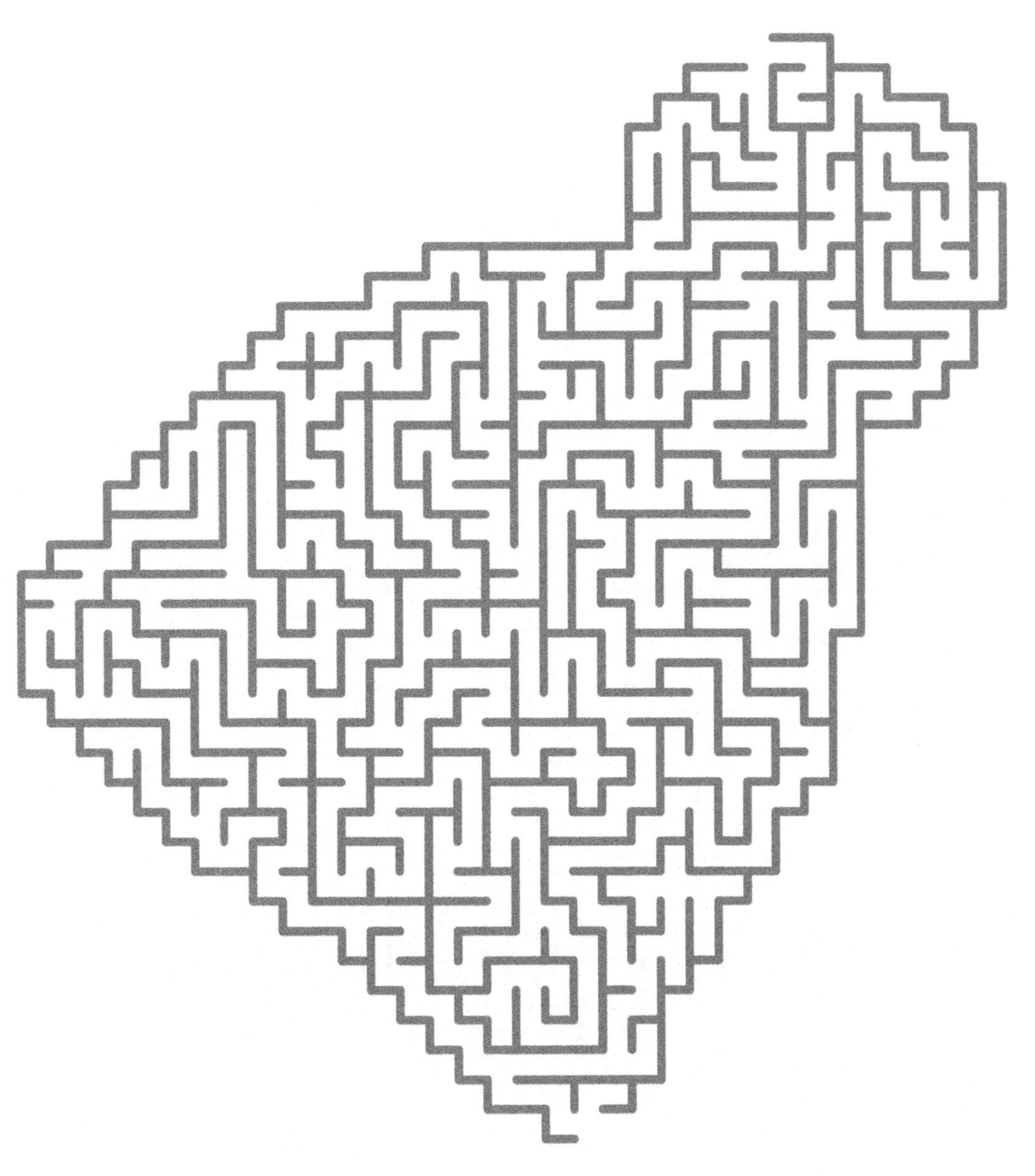

MAZE #26

MAZE #27

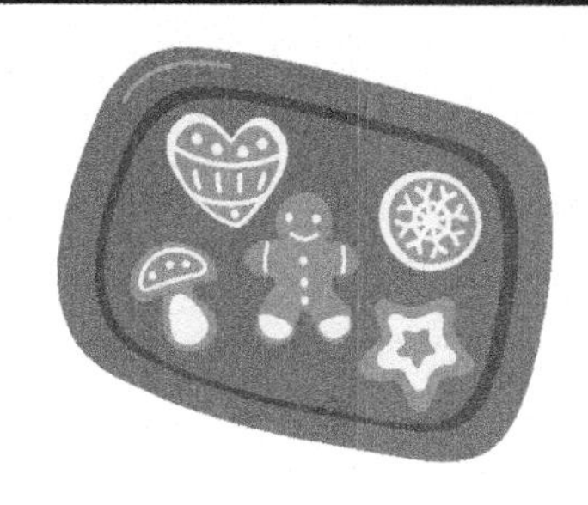

MAZE #28

MAZE #29

MAZE #30

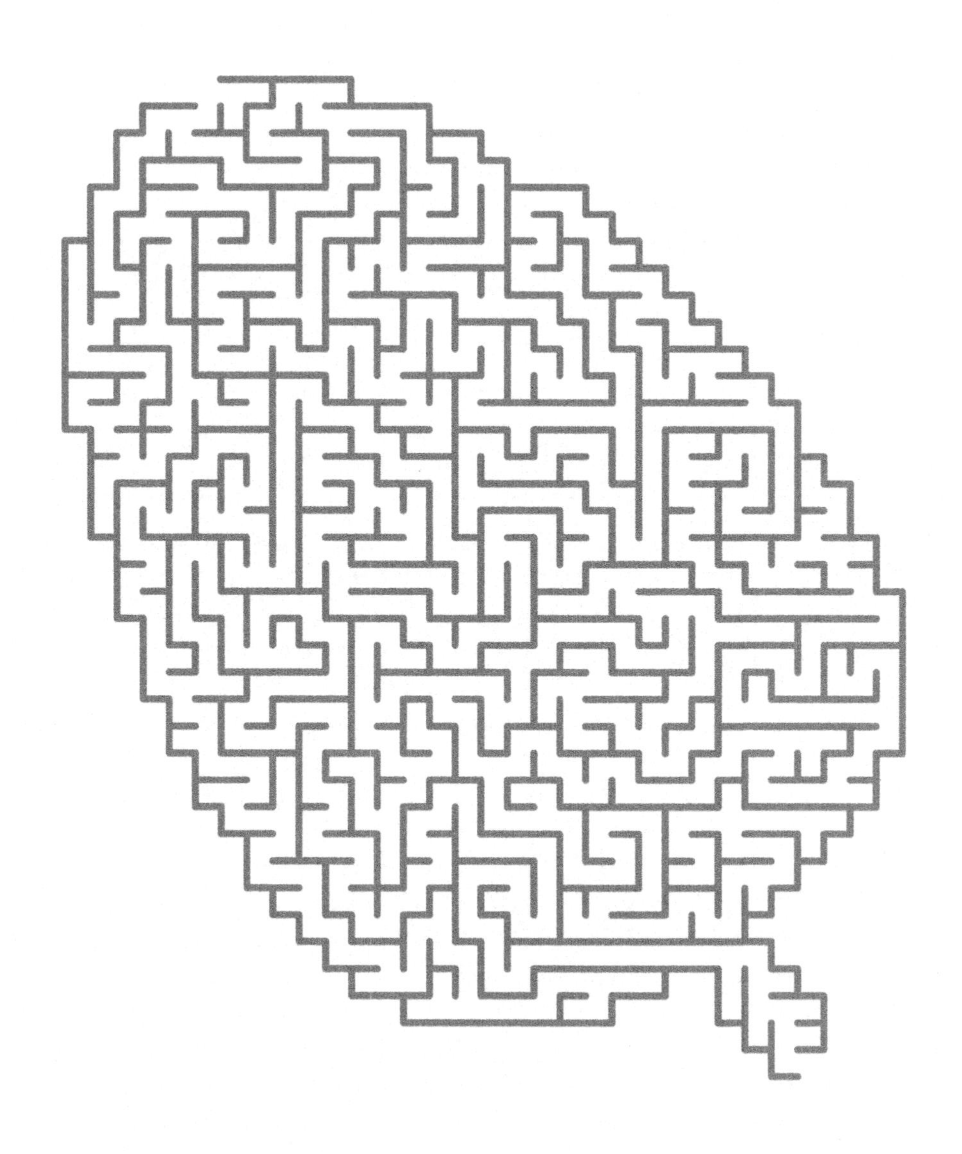

MAZE #31

MAZE #32

MAZE #33

MAZE #34

MAZE #35

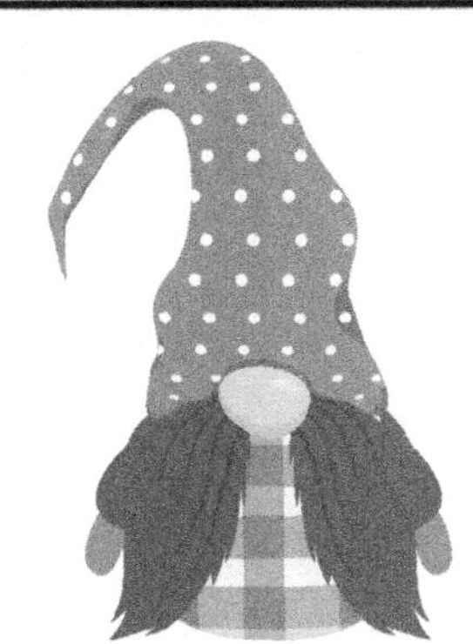

MAZE #36

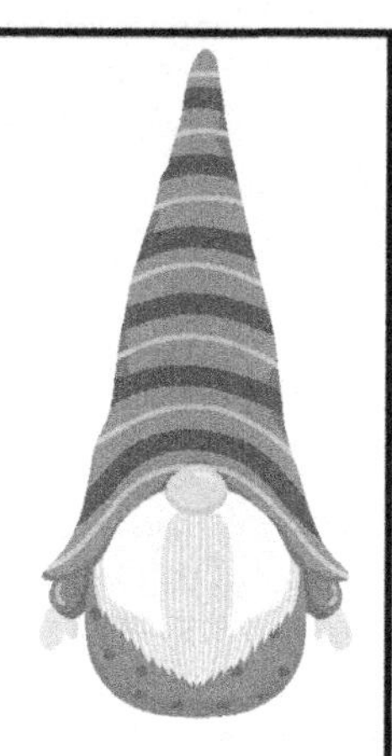

MAZE #37

MAZE #38

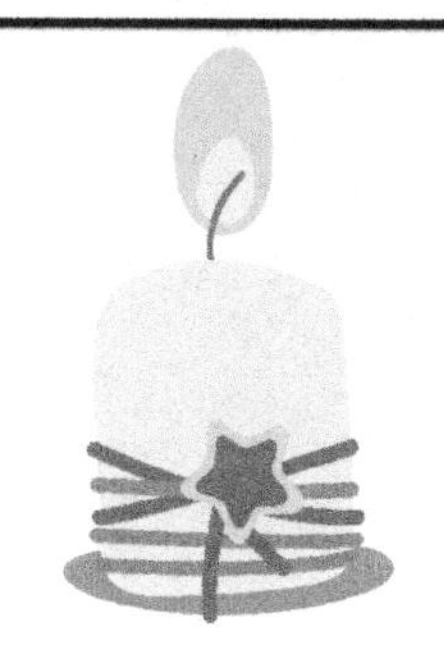

MAZE #39

MAZE #40

MAZE #41

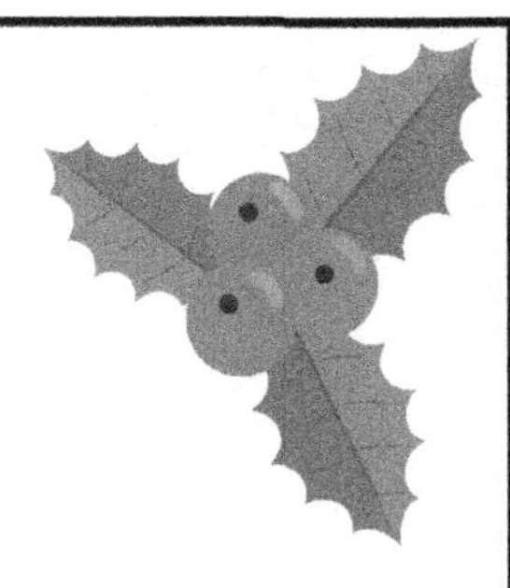

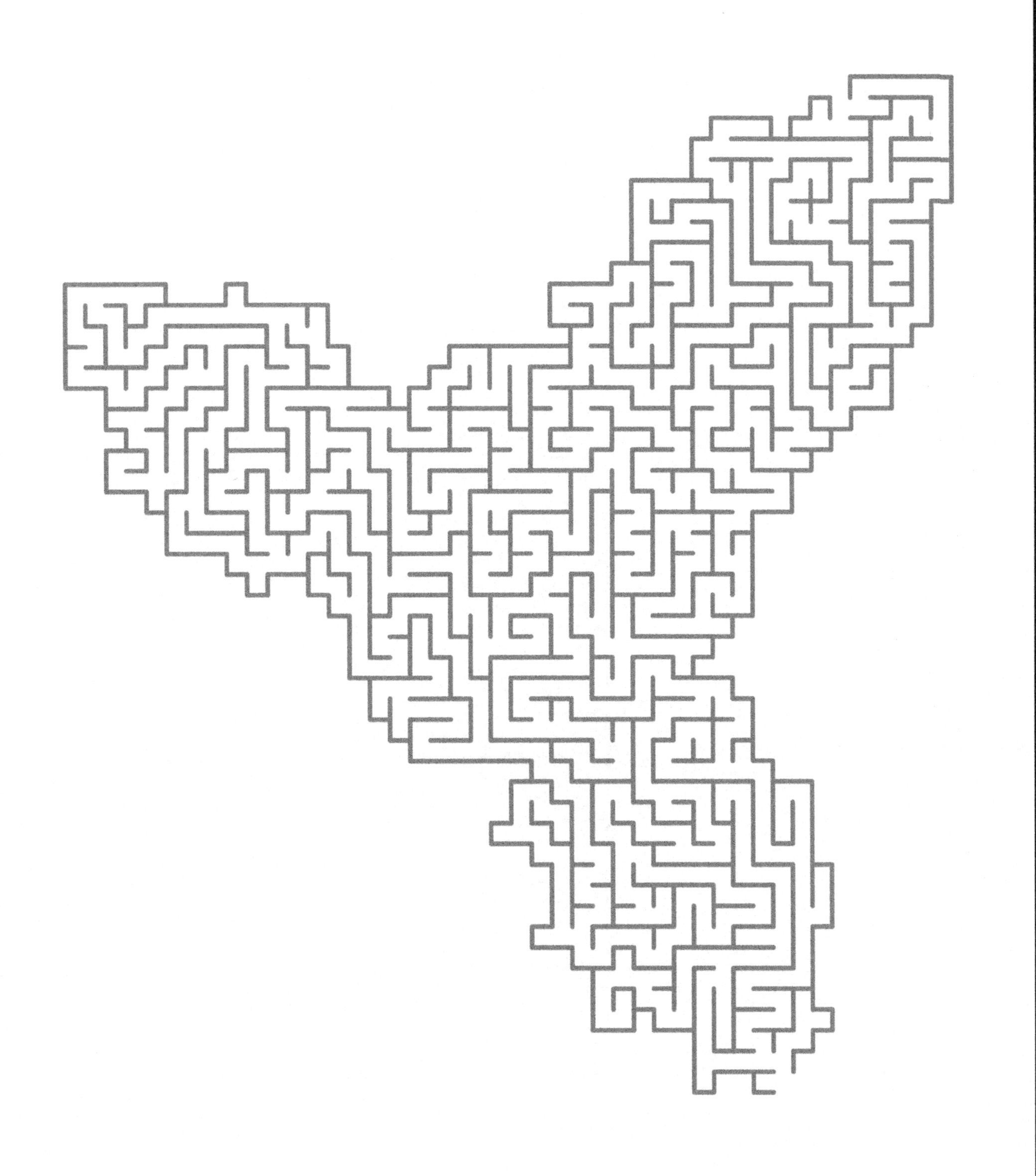

MAZE #42

MAZE #43

MAZE #44

MAZE #45

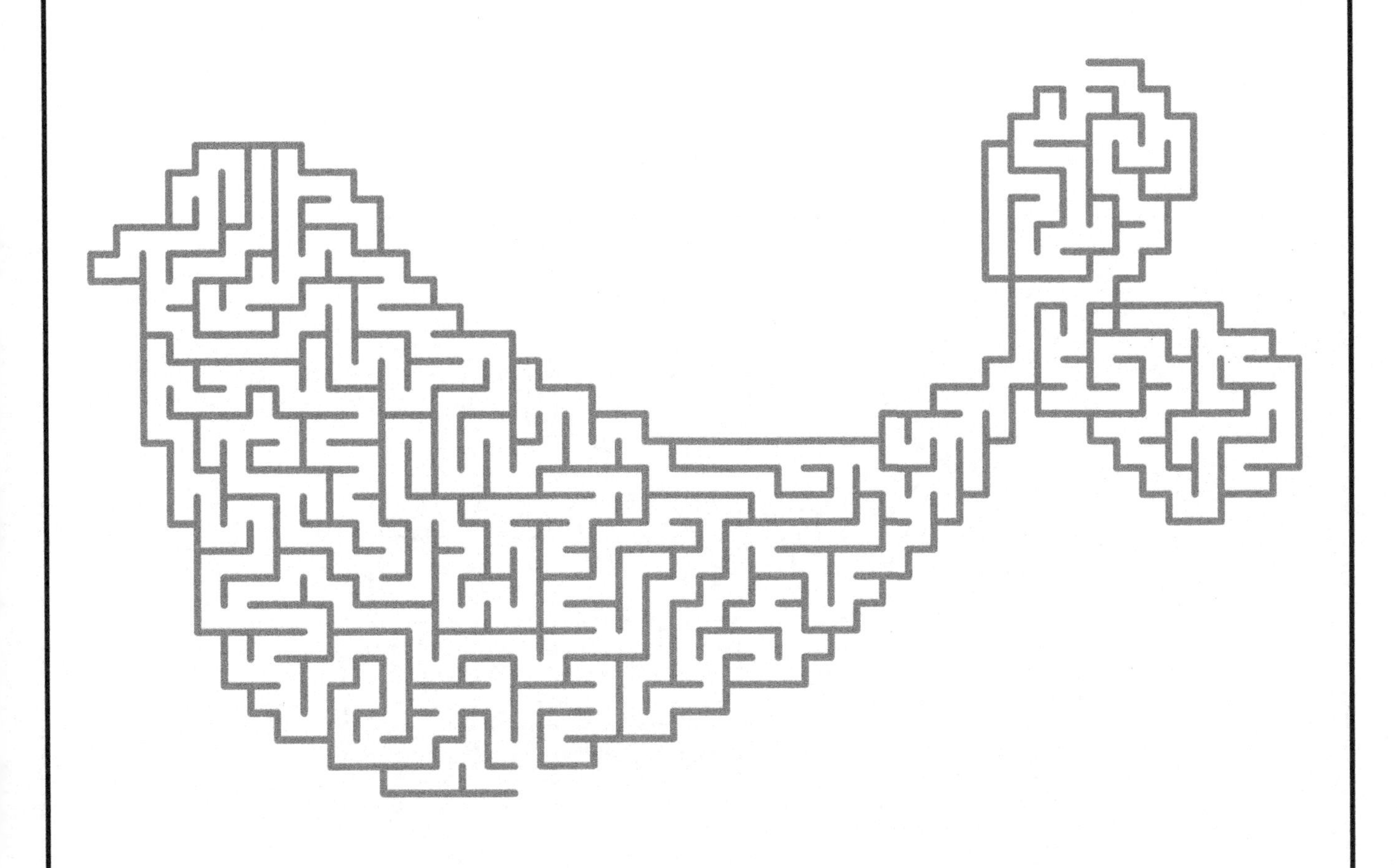

MAZE #46

MAZE #47

MAZE #48

MAZE #49

MAZE #50

COLOR *and* COUNT

CHRISTMAS

_____ _____ _____ _____

_____ _____ _____ _____

Dec

COLOR *and* COUNT

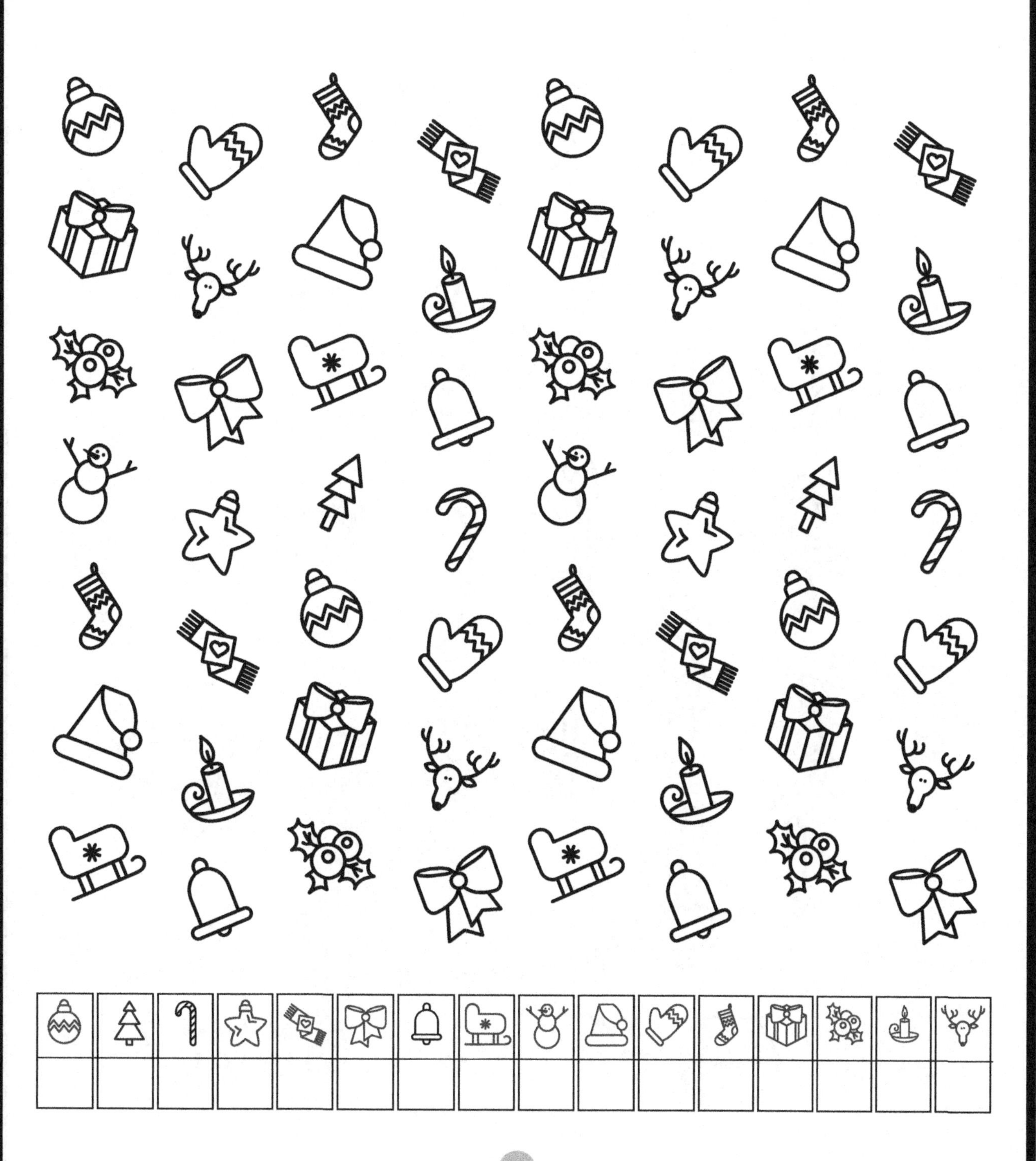

Dec
SALE

COLOR *and* COUNT

Count, color and circle groups of 4 Christmas elements. How many groups do you have? Do all elements belong to a group?

COLOR

HOW MANY SANTAS DO YOU SEE?

Merry Christmas

HOW MANY SANTAS DO YOU SEE?

HOW MANY SANTAS DO YOU SEE?

CHRISTMAS
STOCKING SNOWGLOBE PRESENT
SANTA SNOWMAN DEER
S N O W M A N
C S T O P R S
S N O C H E A
D E W K R S N
S E G I I E T
T R L N G N A
M A O B E T S
FLOUR
HOW MANY SNOWFLAKES?
I spy
WORDSCRAMBLE
GINSTOCK
SMANNOW
YENMICH
SPOT 5 DIFFERENCES

HOW MANY SANTAS DO YOU SEE?

CHRISTMAS
SPOT 5 DIFFERENCES
1 green
2 yellow
3 orange
4 red
5 blue
6 pink
I spy
FIND 7 STARS

FIND 10 DIFFERENCES

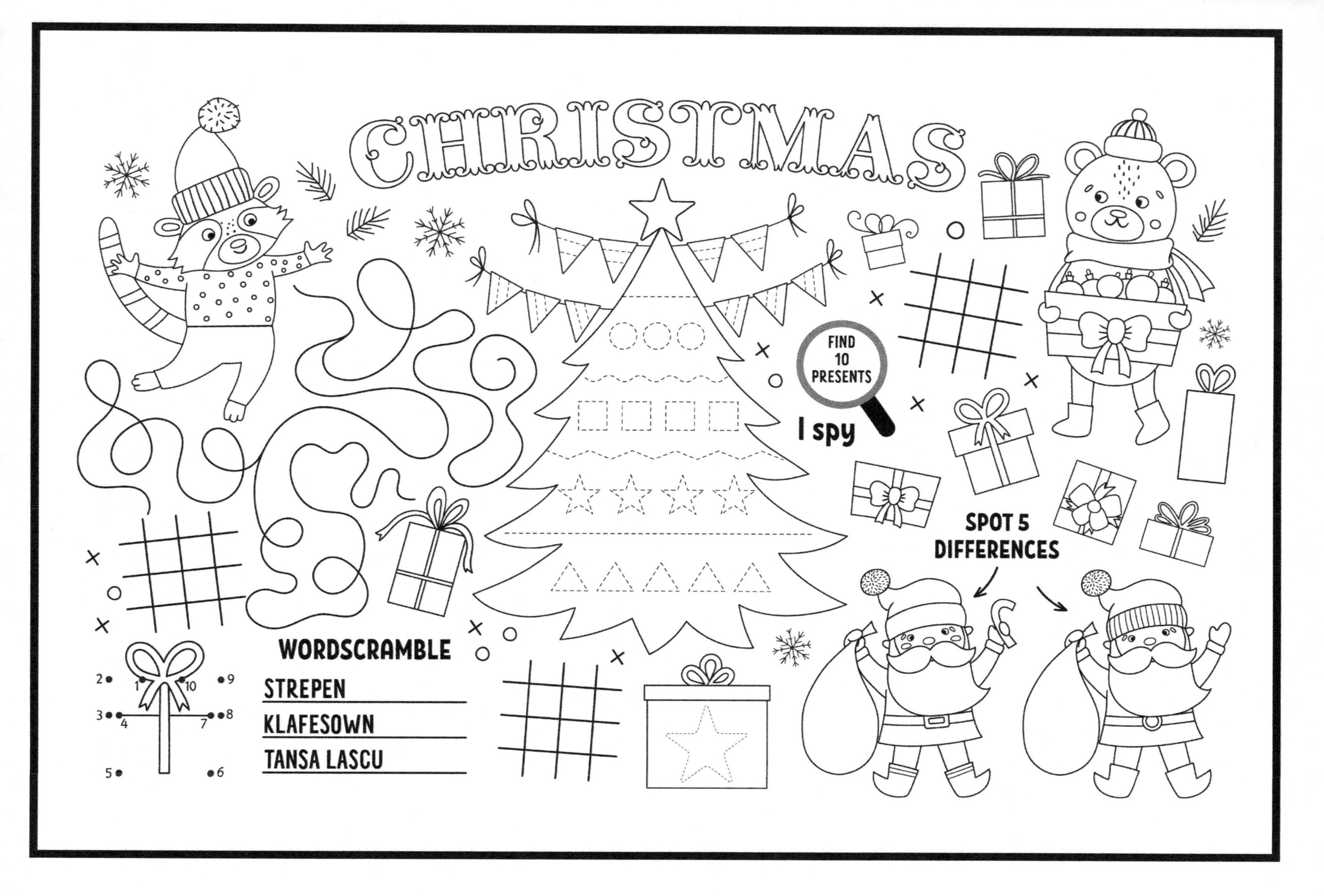
CHRISTMAS
FIND 10 PRESENTS
I spy
SPOT 5 DIFFERENCES
WORDSCRAMBLE
STREPEN
KLAFESOWN
TANSA LASCU
1 2 3 4 5 6 7 8 9 10

FIND 7 DIFFERENCES

SOLUTIONS

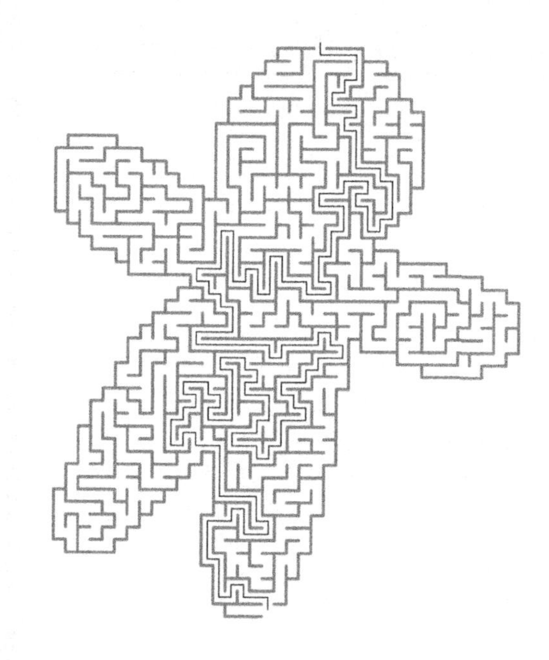

MAZE #1

MAZE #2

MAZE #3

MAZE #4

FIND 7 DIFFERENCES

SOLUTIONS

MAZE #5

MAZE #6

MAZE #7

MAZE #8

FIND 10 DIFFERENCES

SOLUTIONS

MAZE #9

MAZE #10

MAZE #11

MAZE #12

FIND 10 DIFFERENCES

SOLUTIONS

MAZE #13

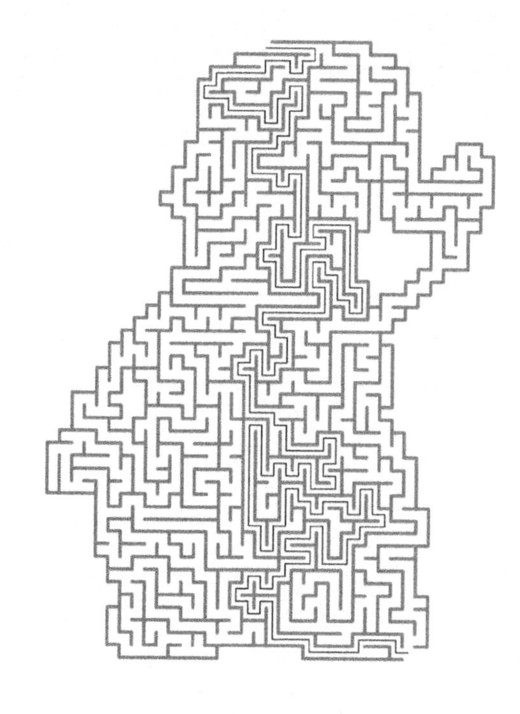

MAZE #14

MAZE #15

MAZE #16

FIND 10 DIFFERENCES

SOLUTIONS

MAZE #17

MAZE #18

MAZE #19

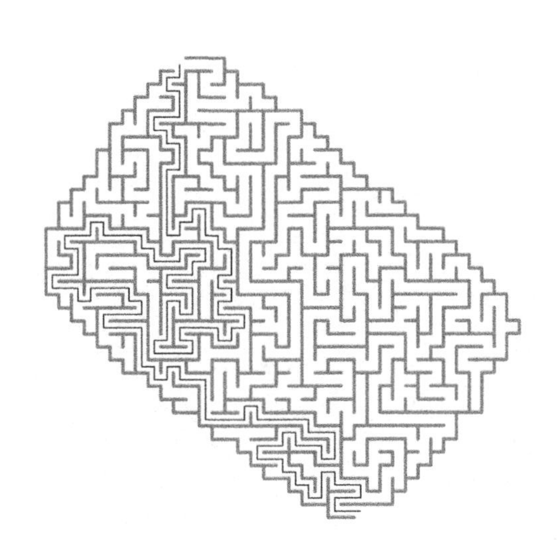

MAZE #20

FIND 10 DIFFERENCES

SOLUTIONS

MAZE #21

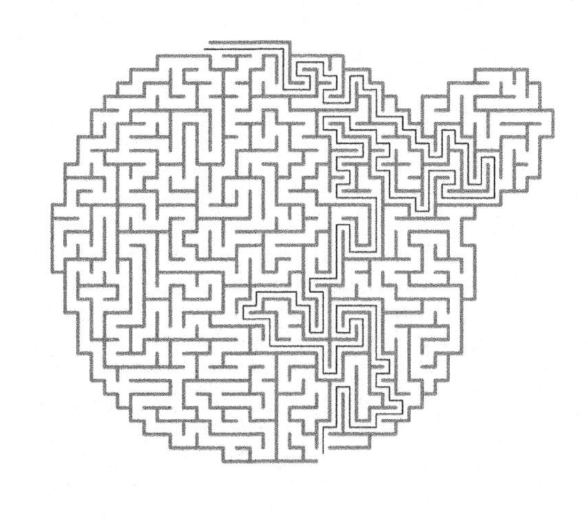

MAZE #22

MAZE #23

MAZE #24

FIND 10 DIFFERENCES

SOLUTIONS

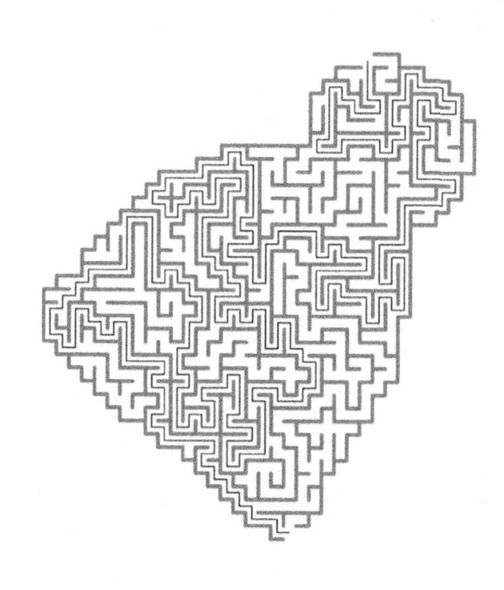

MAZE #25

MAZE #26

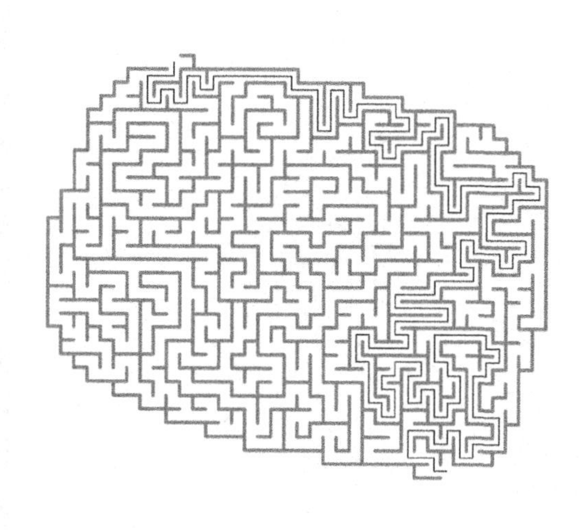

MAZE #27

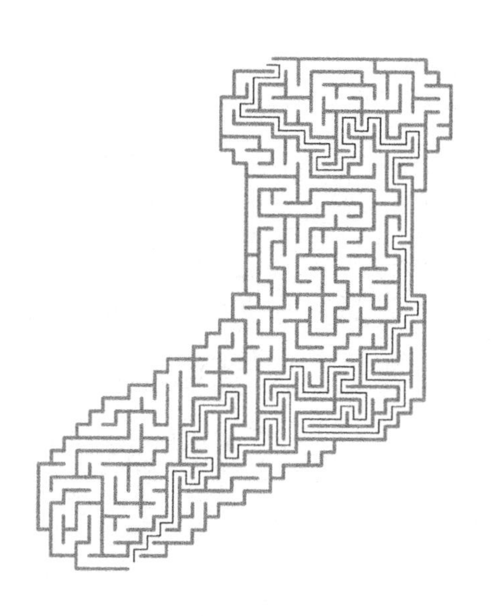

MAZE #28

FIND ONE OF A KIND

SOLUTIONS

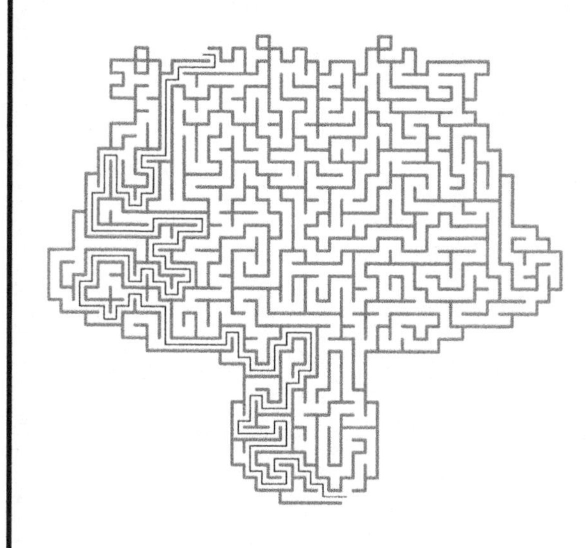

MAZE #29

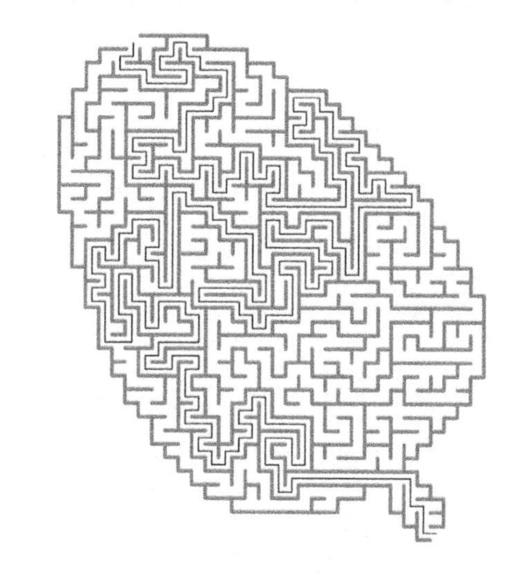

MAZE #30

MAZE #31

MAZE #32

FIND ONE OF A KIND

SOLUTIONS

MAZE #33

MAZE #34

MAZE #35

MAZE #36

FIND ONE OF A KIND

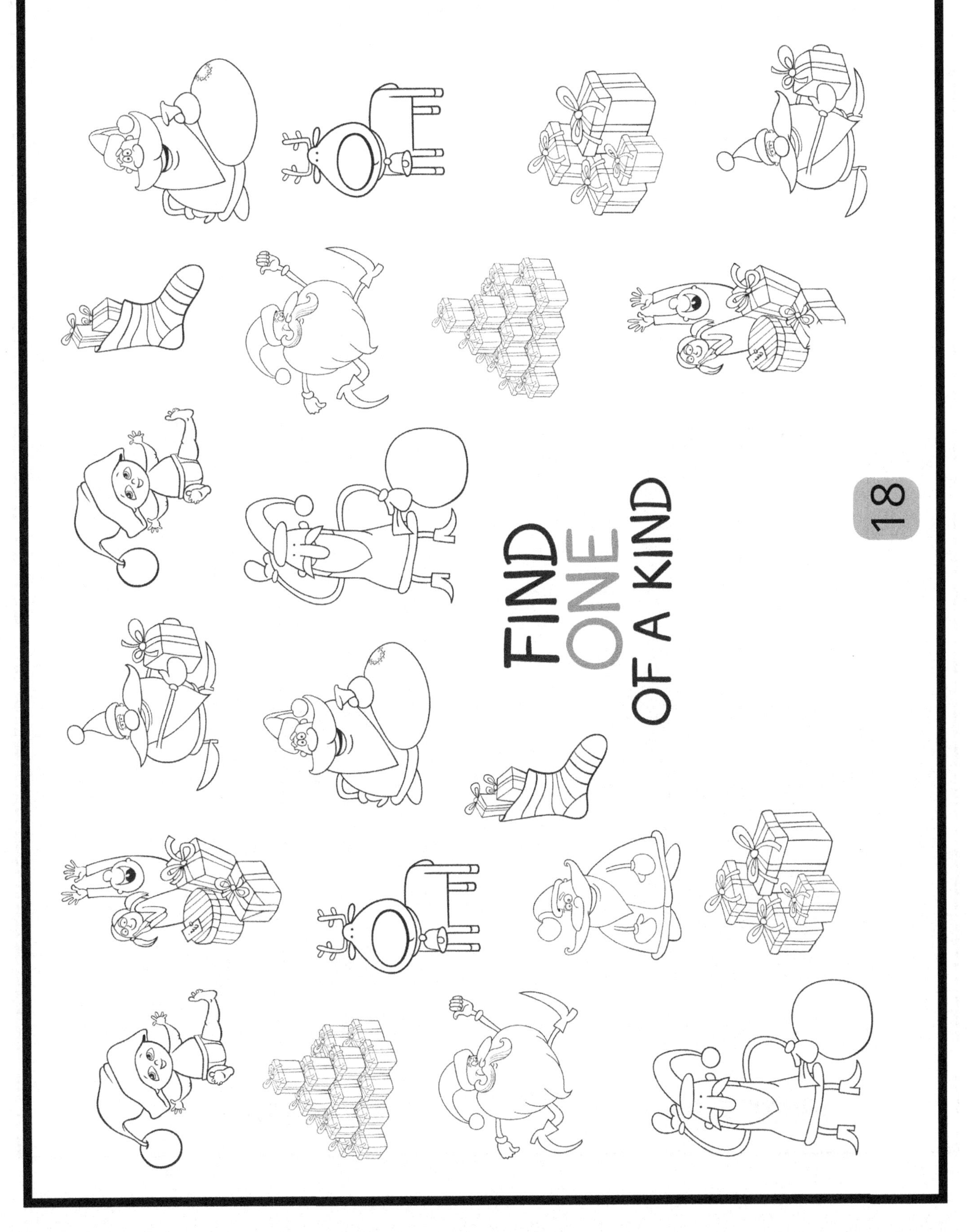

SOLUTIONS

MAZE #37

MAZE #38

MAZE #39

MAZE #40

FIND ONE OF A KIND

SOLUTIONS

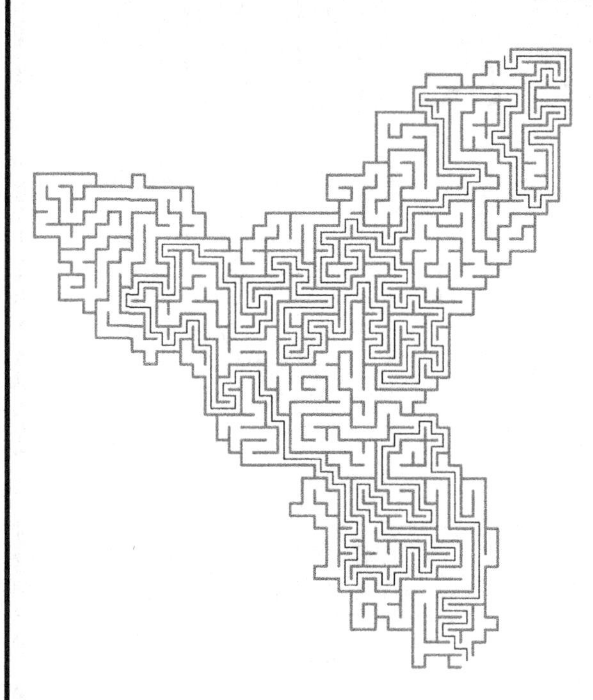

MAZE #41

MAZE #42

MAZE #43

MAZE #44

FIND TWO THE SAME

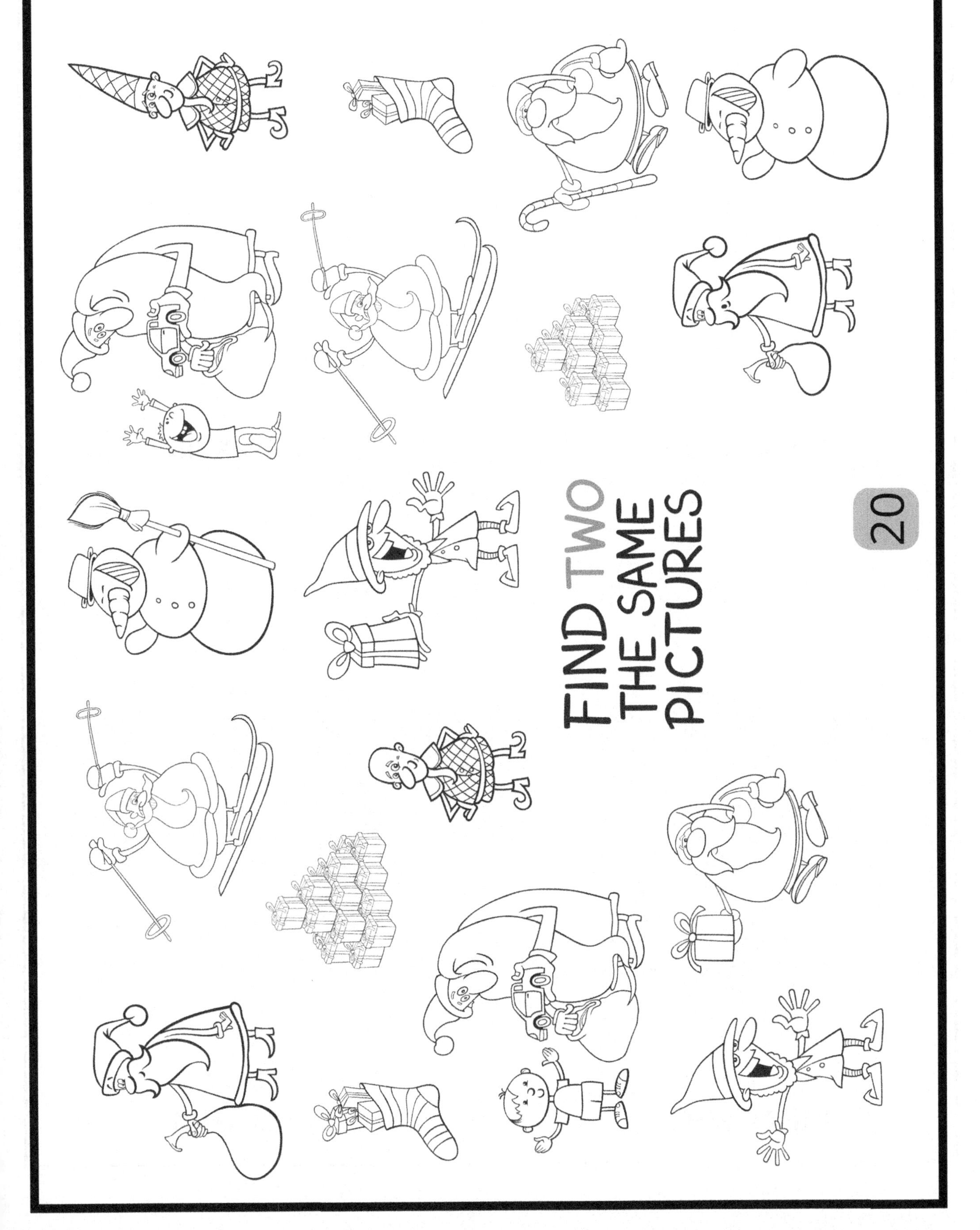

SOLUTIONS

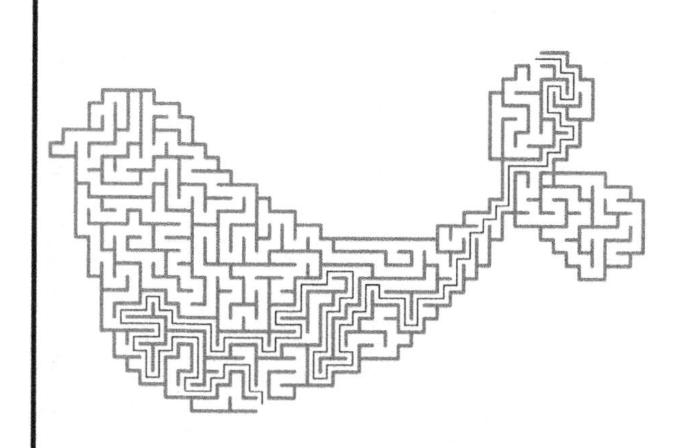

MAZE #45

MAZE #46

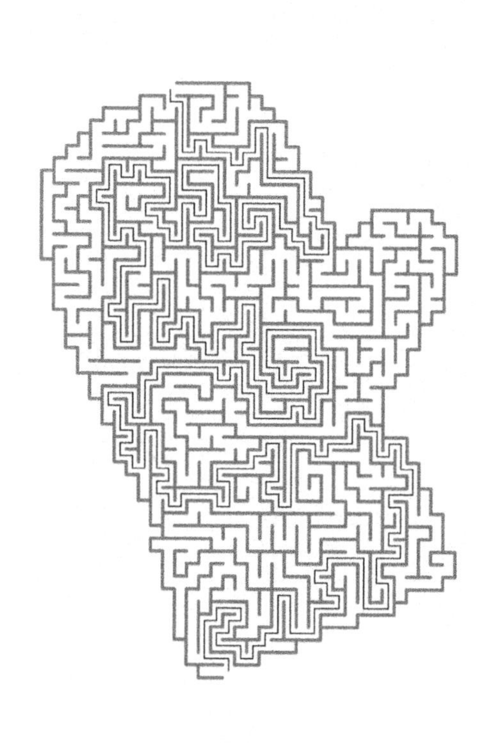

MAZE #47

MAZE #48

FIND TWO THE SAME

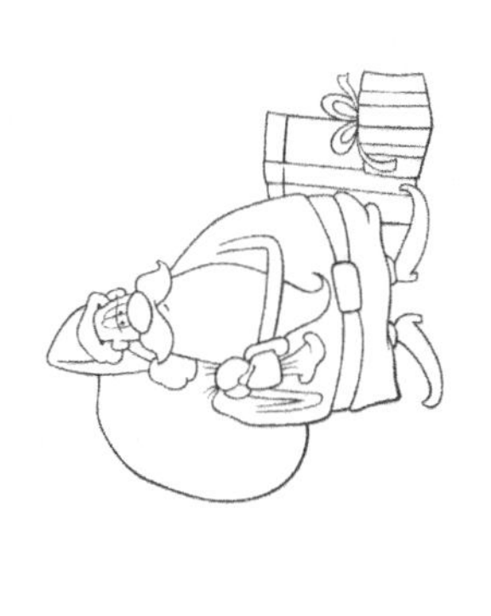
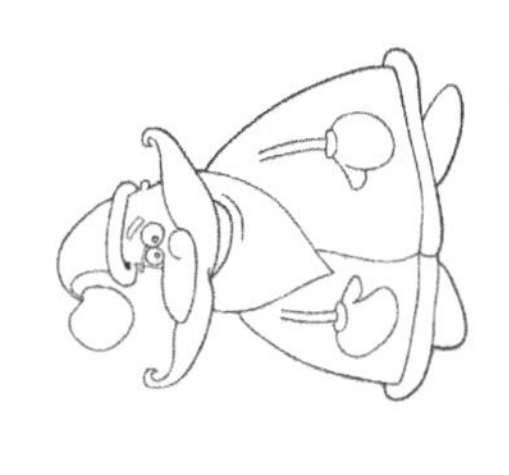
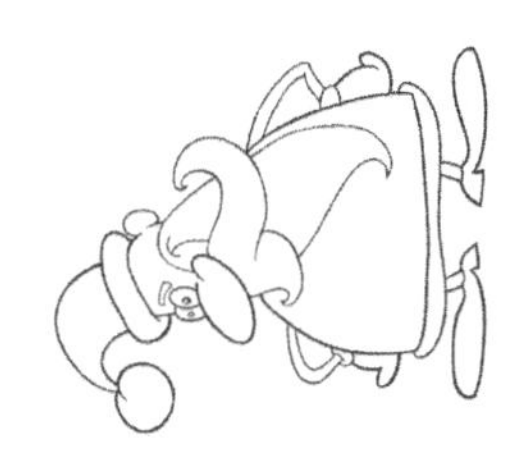

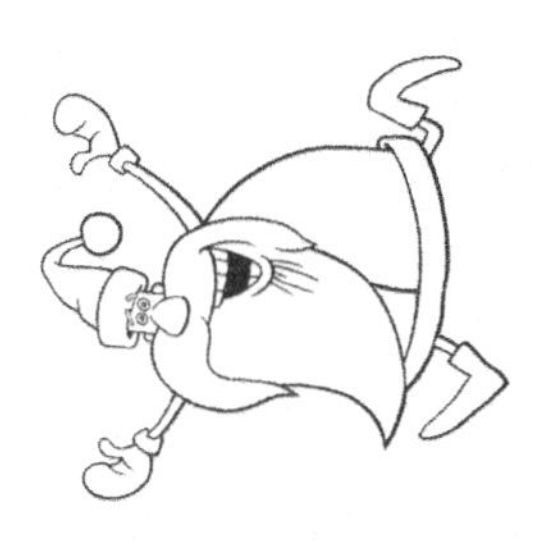

FIND TWO THE SAME PICTURES

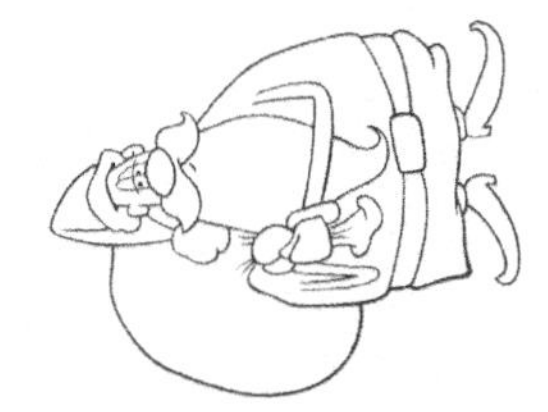

SOLUTIONS

MAZE #49

MAZE #50

FIND TWO THE SAME

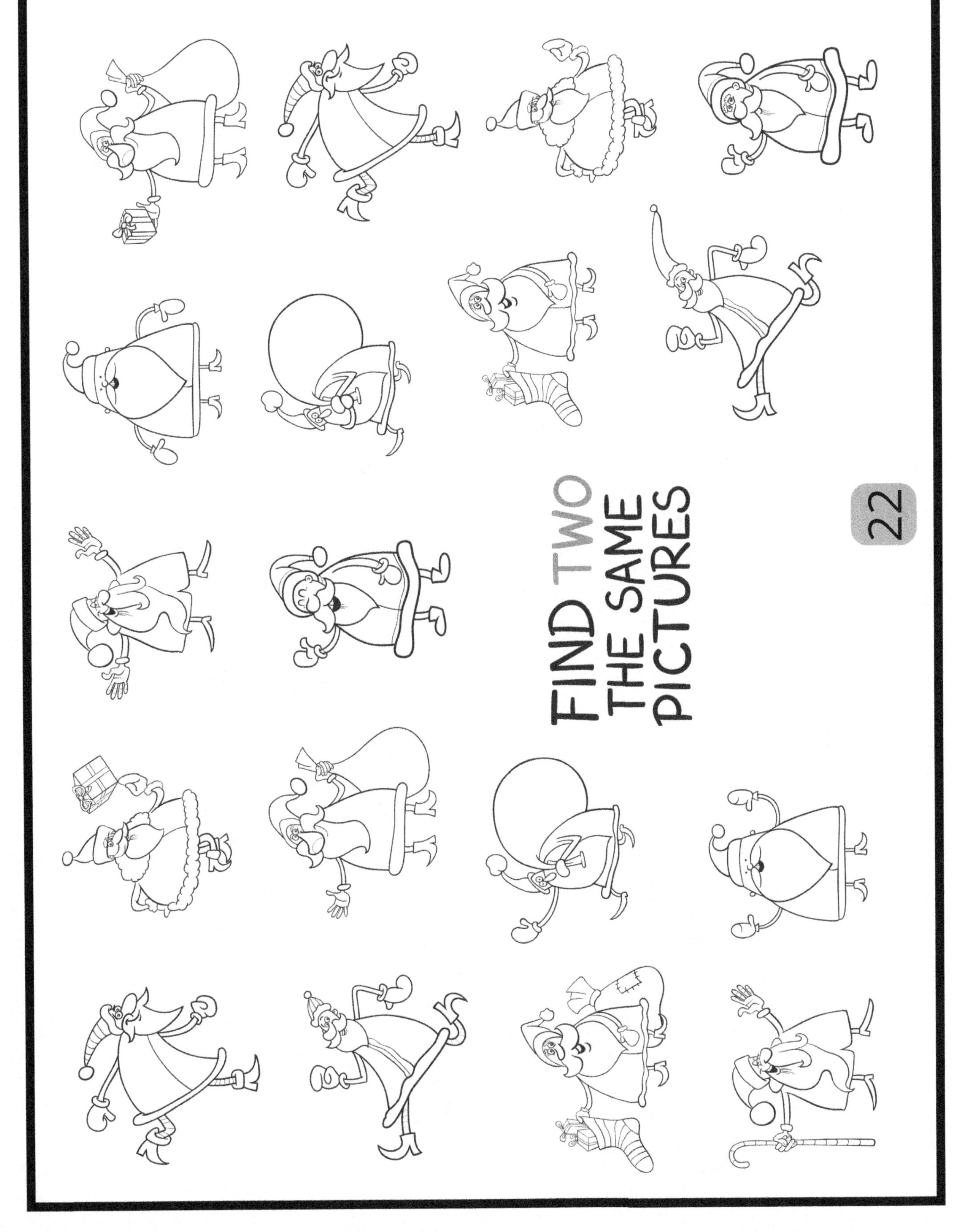

Solutions

(How many Santas do you see?)

4 - 10

5 - 11

6 - 17

7 - 18

Solutions

10

11

12

Solutions

13

14

15

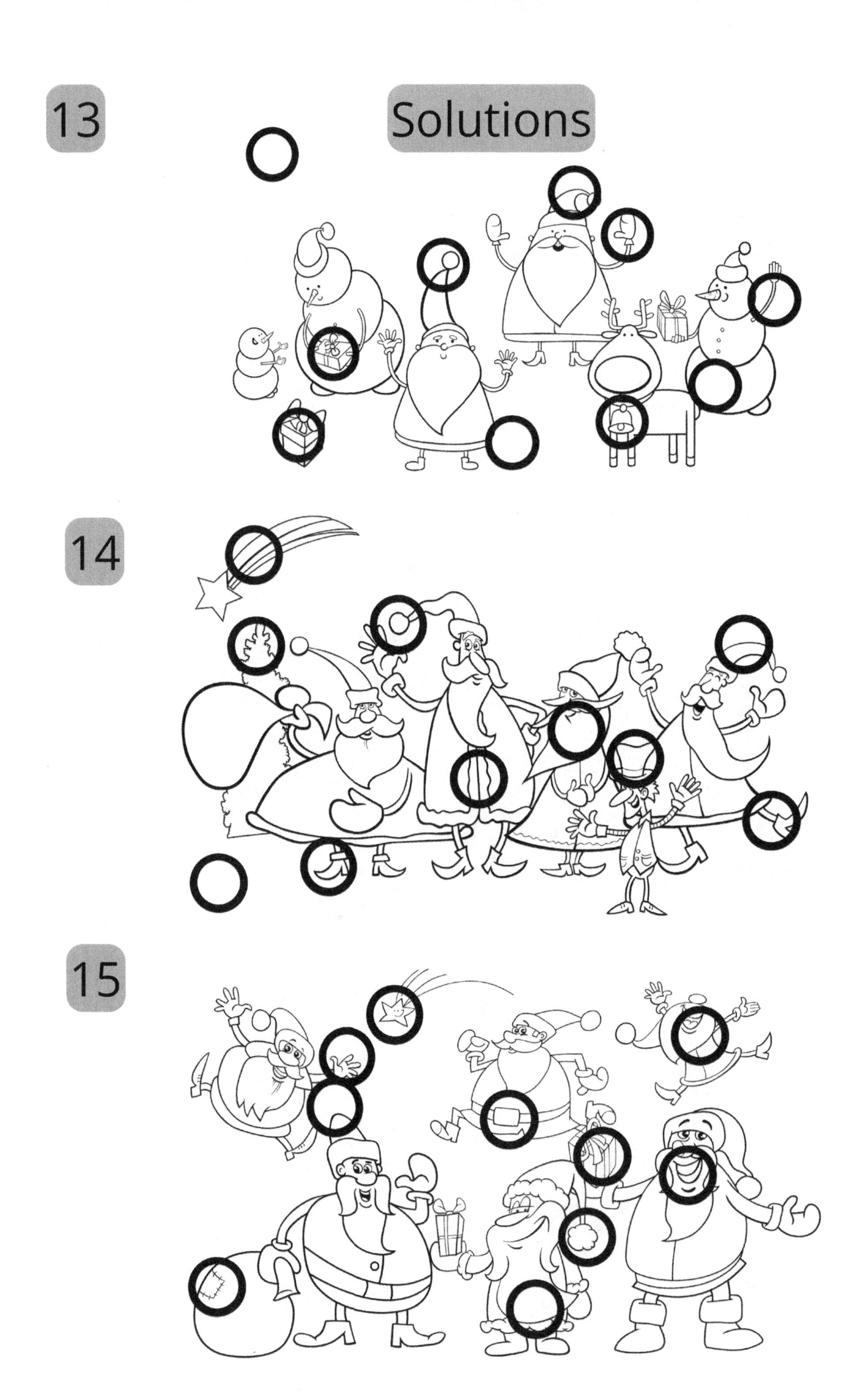

Solutions

16

17

18

19

20

21

22

Made in the USA
Middletown, DE
17 December 2022